This is not intended as a guide book but is a collection of images amassed over 40 odd years of walking, climbing and looking at Nevis from our window.

By Nevis I mean the collective area of Hill, Glen and River which covers many square kilometres of the most scenic countryside anyone could wish for.

Many people are working hard to preserve the beauty of Nevis and hopefully this set of pictures will go some way to help.

Alex. Gillespie

When I think of my old friend Alex Gillespie, I think of Nevis. I guess all of us have our favourite haunts but few of us have those areas implanted in our soul. Alex does, as a mountaineer, as a rescuer, as a fellow gangrel and most importantly as a photographer.

And it's in the outworking of his professional life that you can begin to see, appreciate and understand this connection he has cultivated with Nevis, the hill, the glen and the river.

The Nevis Partnership seeks to protect the natural wonders of this place and this book paints those scenes vividly. It will be a vital tool in our efforts to help people enjoy, appreciate and protect one of the most marvellous corners of Scotland.

Cameron McNeish
The Nevis Partnership

Alex has captured images of this magnificent landscape and some of the wild creatures that share their habitats with the people who live here or visit from afar.

Global weather changes demand that we humans increase our awareness and understanding of this very special area to ensure we cherish and nurture the mountain, its soils, waters and the biodiversity that depends on our stewardship.

This selection of beautiful and compelling photographs are the work of an individual who cares deeply about his home environment. The pictures tell a story that words could never convey.

Tomorrow go for a walk on the hill, in the woodland or by the burn and marvel at the wonders that nature has bestowed on this truly magical mountain.

Dick Balharrie
John Muir Trust

With sheep and cattle grazing and less traditional activities such as today's modern tourism scene and some environmental work, what we do brings about gradual influences on Glen Nevis. An active, majestic landscape of great rugged beauty with changing patterns of grazing and tree cover, many compliment us on the balance achieved.

I have spent all my working life in Glen Nevis and Alex Gillespie has been part of that, photographing and scaling the heights for as long as I can remember. It is a joy to meet Alex and his wife Mary either in or high above the Glen on a fine day.

In his book, Alex brings out views of many of my favourite places in original and exciting ways. I hope you enjoy it as much as I do.

Ewen Cameron
Glen Nevis Estate

DUN DEARDAIL

Grey Corries and Nevis from Gairlochy

Nevis and Aonach Mor from Loch Eil

NEVIS GORGE

purple saxifrage

the prince

steall falls in spate

due east of the ben

on the mamores

summer into autumn

winter into spring

HEADING FOR THE HILL

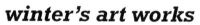

winter's art works

west

east

THE WHISKY BURN

otherwise the Alt na Mhuilinn

BEN NEVIS
DISTILLERY

outflow

the source

nearing the distillery

the spirit safe

the still room

waterslide
above
the glen

water sculpted

winter garb

leaving the summit

*deciding on which
route to take*

we climbed the ben

SURVIVAL HUT
Lifted from Corpach to this site
by
RAF WESSEX SAR HELICOPTER
on
29 September 1991

Crew:
ROBIN SLADDEN   PAUL DOWELL

BEN NEVIS
SUMMIT
1344mtrs

BEN NEVIS
SUMMIT
4406ft

TREE ROOT SYSTEM

UPPPER GLEN NEVIS

HELP

LOCHABER MOUNTAIN RESCUE TEAM

FOR ALMOST 30 YEARS THE LOCHABER MOUNTAIN RESCUE TEAM RAN A FUND-RAISING
RIVER RACE WHICH IS NOW ABANDONED DUE TO ORGANISATIONAL PROBLEMS AND A
LACK OF WATER IN AUGUST, PROBABLY CAUSED BY GLOBAL WARMING ?

SOFT CONDITIONS   **HARD CONDITIONS**

(private)